COMING HOME
IN VIET NAM

BOOKS BY EDWARD TICK

NONFICTION

The Future of Ancient Healing: A Journey into the Roots and Spirit of Psychology and Medicine, forthcoming 2022

Warrior's Return: Restoring the Soul After War, 2014

War and the Soul: Healing Our Nation's Veterans from Post-Traumatic Stress Disorder, 2005

The Practice of Dream Healing: Bringing Ancient Greek Mysteries into Modern Medicine, 2001

Sacred Mountain: Encounters with the Vietnam Beast, 1989

POETRY

The Bull Awakening: Poetry of Crete and Santorini, 2016

The Golden Tortoise: Viet Nam Journeys, 2005

MONOGRAPH

Wild Beasts and Wandering Souls: Shamanism and Post-Traumatic Stress Disorder, 2007

AUDIO

Restoring the Warrior's Soul: An Essential Guide to Coming Home, 2016

COMING HOME
IN VIET NAM

POEMS BY
EDWARD TICK

Printed in the United States.
ISBN: 978-1-882688-60-9

Book Design: Jane Brunette

Cover art: Ut Quyen

Published by:
Tià Chucha Press
A project of Tià Chucha's Centro Cultural, Inc.
PO Box 328
San Fernando, CA 91341
tiachucha.org

Distributed by:
Northwestern University Press
Chicago Distribution Center
11030 South Langley Avenue Chicago IL 60628

Tià Chucha's Centro Cultural & Bookstore is a 501 (c) (3) nonprofit corporation funded in part over the years by the Arts for Justice Fund, National Endowment for the Arts, California Arts Council, Los Angeles County Arts Commission, Los Angeles Department of Cultural Affairs, The California Community Foundation, the Annenberg Foundation, the Weingart Foundation, the Lia Fund, National Association of Latino Arts and Culture, Ford Foundation, MetLife, Southwest Airlines, the Andy Warhol Foundation for the Visual Arts, the Thrill Hill Foundation, the Middleton Foundation, Center for Cultural Innovation, John Irvine Foundation, Not Just Us Foundation, Liberty Hill Foundation, the Attias Family Foundation, and the Guacamole Fund, Arts for Justice Fund, among others. Donations have also come from Bruce Springsteen, John Densmore of The Doors, Jackson Browne, Lou Adler, Richard Foos, Gary Stewart, Charles Wright, Adrienne Rich, Tom Hayden, Dave Marsh, Jack Kornfield, Jesus Trevino, David Sandoval, Gary Soto, Sandra Cisneros, Denise Chavez and John Randall of the Border Book Festival, Luis & Trini Rodriguez, and others.

Contents

9. *KIM QUY*: THE GOLDEN TORTOISE

The Tale of King Le Loi

Gratitude

Tran Dinh Song has been my in-country guide, teacher, and co-leader on every annual journey I have led since my first trip in 2000. He is a teacher, healer, and my brother. His wife Huyen Thi Lan is our dear friend and loving hostess.

I met my god-daughter Nguyen Thi Ngoc in 2005 at the 995th anniversary of Ha Noi's founding. She interviewed me then for her college newspaper and has since opened profound doors to intimacy. She says, "Please keep bringing your vets here so I can heal them with my love."

I met my god-niece Pham Ut Quyen, Ngoc's dear friend, soon after. She has been on our journeys, helped our healing work, translated for us, contributed the cover art, and now sings to our veterans.

Lam Van Tien, "Tam," is a Viet Cong veteran who hosts my groups every year since we met two decades ago. Severely wounded during the war, he has opened his humble Delta home and huge heart to frightened GIs. He says, "American and Vietnamese veterans must be the lips and tongue of the same mouth telling the world the same story."

Huỳnh Ngoc Vân is the retired director of the War Remnants Museum and now co-directs the Ao Dai Museum, both in Ho Chi Minh City. Together we have conducted peace and healing programs for international reconciliation through art and ceremony in both countries.

Huu Ngoc, a former Viet Minh and Viet Cong, is a century-old writer, scholar, and educator. A distinguished elder, he has welcomed and taught my groups every year and brought my work into Viet Nam through some of his own writings and by republishing mine. He has been a *thay*, a revered teacher and mentor, to me and countless others.

Nguyen Tam Ho, "Mr. Tiger," was at war for 25 years and then worked for peace and land renewal for the half century following. He and his son Nhiep welcomed, taught, blessed, and helped heal our groups during every visit to the Mekong Delta. May he rest in peace.

Dr. Lê Văn Hao and Director Dr. Lã Thu Thoy of the Institute of Psychology, Ngoc and Phuong's families, Hoàng Minh Nhân and Pham Si Man of Da Nang Street Children's Center, Col. Đặng Vương Hưng and Soldier's Heart Viet Nam, Dr. Tang, Prof. Minh Thai, Hua Lu, my sculptor nephew Son in Hoi An, my favorite English teacher in the world Sapa of Tam Ky Elementary School, Tony Hai, so many others... In Viet Nam these relationships are truer than blood and honored as family, because they are chosen, enduring, and responsible for each other and the shared mission of healing our two countries and creating *hoa binh*, peace.

I thank Prof. Stephen Leibo, with whom I partnered to lead our first few return journeys and teach our findings together at The Sage Colleges.

I especially honor and thank every veteran and traveler over the decades who has had the courage, open mind, heart, and determination to join these journeys to heal self and contribute to healing survivors from both sides and both countries. And especially the Vietnamese people, who provide our healing ecology. They are universally kind, caring, welcoming, forgiving, and devoted to peace and friendship.

Thanks to Luis J. Rodriguez for his guiding vision for Tia Chucha Press to heal and reconcile cultures and peoples, especially through poetry, and for welcoming this project. Thanks to Miguel Rivera for partnering with me for years providing cross-cultural men's healing work and for introducing this work to Luis and serving as midwife.

Finally, and always, I thank and honor my wife, work and life partner Kate Dahlstedt. Kate has co-led a decade of journeys to Viet Nam. She has been instrumental in our healing work in both nations and especially supportive and proactive in helping women and children wounded by war everywhere. Kate is an eternal and loving source of support, understanding, compassion and generosity in this international war-healing and reconciliation mission we share.

I am grateful to my translators and to the editors of these publications:

"Long Haired Warrior," *Simply Haiku*, Spring 2005.

"Rush Hour," "Tuyen," "Massage Girl I & II", "Cyclo Driver," "My Lai Guide I & II," "The Legend of King Le Loi" in original

I am only a simple farmer,
but I have learned this
from my lifetime of trials and losses:
as life flows on and on
everything disappears except love.

ANH HAT
ELDERLY DISABLED VETERAN
NORTHERN VIETNAMESE COUNTRYSIDE

Introduction

WAR—ARMED CONFLICTS END, and history records them as over. But in the minds, hearts, souls, and wounded bodies of the people who survived, wars go on and on. The land that suffered war bears scars for decades or longer. The generations that follow bear their impact and show ongoing wounds. We seek to end wars but do not know how to stop its personal and transgenerational damage.

Though never having served in the military, I have been passionately protesting the ordeal of my generation, what Americans call the Vietnam War and its aftermath, my entire adult life. I judged it as wrong, immoral, misdirected when I began protesting in high school. I ached for both our troops and the Vietnamese people. I did not believe the political myths and spin that sought to justify it. I watched it tear our country and my generation apart in ways that have not yet healed. I grieved the waste.

Shortly after the war's end in 1975, as a young psychotherapist, I began working with alienated, lost, hurting veterans. This was before the psychological diagnosis of Post-Traumatic Stress Disorder (PTSD), created in 1980, gave a name to the invisible wound of war that has, in fact, been known since ancient times. When a young veteran walked into my office, I looked at a man who was my age but already used up. I thought, as Phil Ochs sang at the time, "There but for fortune go you or I." It could have been me. Since I did not have to serve during the war, working to heal our invisibly wounded warriors as a "homefront doc" became my alternative service. I did not then know that this work would become my lifelong calling to our troubled nation and my generation, shredded by this misguided adventure. I did not know that I would specialize in military and veteran matters, that I would gain much from this service to tend wounded warriors and civilians from various wars, that American wars would go on and on, and that I would also serve the Vietnamese people and country in healing. I was propelled onto a life path and destiny.

THOUGH TECHNICALLY NOT A VETERAN, I have been welcomed by veterans into their brotherhood, for I have been drenched in that war, its stories and suffering, its hardships and blessings, its tears of grief and relief for over forty years now. A friend said to me recently, "Imagine what your life would have been like if you had gone to Viet Nam." The irony – protesting that war and hating its pain, lies, betrayal, and duplicity, I have served its aftermath my entire adult life and that service has transformed me into a military and war trauma specialist. I have been serving every American generation and war since.

My passion and commitment that had once been directed in youthful protest against that war became my passionate commitment to heal our veterans and their families and restore a healthy warrior archetype that protects and preserves but does not destroy. The protest movement insisted that our country "bring the boys back home." After the war it was painfully clear: they were not boys and they were not brought home. In my heart and soul I accepted responsibility for our country's moral injury that was not personally mine and for bringing the women and men whose actions I protested all the way home.

I sought every avenue for comprehensive healing of war's invisible wounds. From its creation as a modern diagnostic category, the field of trauma psychology has grown like the many-headed hydra of mythology replicating itself: parades, medications, brain chemistry, eye movement, exposure, cognitive retraining, mindfulness meditation, equine therapy, service dogs, outdoor adventures, free cars and vacations—the list of strategies to respond to violent trauma now seems endless. But what works? What sticks? What brings such deep inner resolution and peace that the nightmares and alienation cease and the heart can heal and love again? I sought that answer.

THERE IS SO MUCH ABOUT WAR TRAUMA that cannot be accessed in the consultation room. Some veterans continued to fear, hate, and misjudge the Vietnamese. Some declared they had been on the wrong side and wished they had fought with them. Most carried what we now call Moral Injury, the deep wound of having done, participated in, witnessed, or just supported from a distance what they judge to be ultimately wrong. Socrates taught that the soul is wounded by wrong-doing. It was not merely their altered brain chemistry. It was their souls that ached to the depths and, no matter how expert the office therapy, could only be taken so far in their homecoming and healing while remaining divorced from both mainstream society at home and the people they felt we had wronged. In their minds, their nightmares, their energies and behaviors, the war was still raging, the jungles and villages still burning.

But how to bring them home? And what about the Vietnamese? What were their stories, their suffering and losses? How did they endure? How did they fare afterwards? How do they feel toward us? Were there endless invisible wounds in their people and culture? Did they need as much or more help recovering as our veterans do?

By the millennium, the quarter-century anniversary of the end of that war, I determined that much greater steps were needed to end those ongoing wars. Encountering the Vietnamese land and people, learning who they truly are, seeing the land recovering and meeting the people decades after the bombs stopped falling, might give us a chance to end the wars within. When I began leading the first of my healing and reconciliation journeys to Viet Nam in 2000, I knew little about the Vietnamese people, land, culture, history, or spirituality. But I needed to know these people and how they endured and finally triumphed. And I needed to discover whether reconciliation was possible and could end the inner wars torturing our survivors.

NOW, MORE THAN TWENTY YEARS AFTER my first annual journey, I have spent more than my year in-country and become as intimate, initiated, and included with the Vietnamese as with my closest, dearest family relations. We have indeed become family. And I dare say that nearly every one of the several hundred American veterans, family members, peace activists, sandbox war veterans, teachers, healers, students, and others I have escorted to Viet Nam have been profoundly changed for the better for having visited and reconciled. Among our veterans who have returned, most say that their PTSD is no more.

Who are the Vietnamese people who successfully resisted not only the American incursion but also two thousand years of invasions and occupations by larger and stronger countries, such as China, Japan, and France? Who are these who do not carry the invisible soul wounds that are endemic among American veterans that we call Post-Traumatic Stress Disorder and Moral Injury? Who are these who instead live in forgiveness and acceptance, and who welcome and offer healing and love to those who invaded and destroyed? And what are their stories that we need to know in order to complete our full human history of that war, to make it one story, to reconcile? How can we bring our wounded veterans the inner peace and contentment that the Vietnamese, in spite of their overwhelming war losses, have achieved?

After decades of therapeutic work and research, I became convinced that our office-bound conventional means and medication-dominated treatments for war trauma do not bring abiding inner peace and healing. Thus for the past twenty years I have led annual reconciliation journeys to Viet Nam. Meeting the former foe, immersing in their culture and spirituality, transforming the "other" into friend and family, sharing stories, grief, and honor together, atoning and rebuilding through philanthropy and service, are all forms of atonement that cleanse the moral injury and free the heart and soul from their devastating entrapment in the experience of war.

My first visit more than twenty years after I began working with traumatized warriors immediately demonstrated that this hope for radical healing could prove true. Our veterans arrive in Viet Nam often expecting blame and hostility, even punishment. They receive only respect, honor, love, and forgiveness. They are told they did no wrong, that they acted as warriors must in their nation's service. Not them but only those who sent them bear responsibility for the wrongdoings.

Beyond this blessed discovery, an unexpected world opened. It was as if the Vietnamese have been waiting for our return. Today, especially in Sai Gon and Ha Noi and among the younger generations born after the war, the Vietnamese devour the businesses and corporations,

investments and consumer goods that come with globaliza-
tion. This has become a new form of Western invasion. But
in the countryside and poor sections of the cites, among tra-
ditional or needy people less touched by the modern world,
the Vietnamese have been waiting to meet, share stories,
and grieve together. As one Viet Cong veteran said to our
group, "I have to know if we ever met before under different
circumstances." And as northern country people have said
to us, "Until your visit, the only Americans we ever met
were your bombs. We want to know you." Every year, every
visit, we are deeply, gratefully, joyously welcomed. Viet-
namese tell our veterans, "We know of your pain and suf-
fering in the U.S. We are sorry you could not heal and come
home in America. Please come home here." Viet Nam and
its people become the greater "consulting room," the heal-
ing ecology in which the soul can be restored.

THE POEMS IN THIS COLLECTION are composed from the
stories I have heard, witnessed, and facilitated over my
twenty years of journeys throughout Viet Nam. There are
three voices in these poems. I tell the Vietnamese people's
stories, often in first person, in the voices of those who ex-
perienced them. They reveal much about the spirituality,
culture, and history of the Viet and indigenous people, and
of their experiences during what they call the American
War and since. Many of these are stories of women, chil-
dren, and non-combatants. We think of wars as the stories
of men in combat and utmost distress. We do not know the
toil, sacrifice, suffering, contributions, and healing of the
women and the innocents. We do not know the effects of a
society forcibly engaged in a "people's war" that impacts ev-
eryone in their own homeland experiences. We do not know
how the women of that society responded to their country's

threat and need. We do not know how to touch and penetrate our wounded warriors' hearts and souls so that they can indeed "come home." We learn all this and more with and from the Vietnamese people.

We hear the voices and experiences of returning American veterans. These journeys are transformational in the healing they bring our wounded warriors yet are hardly known and even difficult to imagine and believe in the United States. Such encounters pass far beyond anything that can be achieved stateside. In the consultation room a veteran can grieve the killing of a foe, an innocent person, the burning of a hut or bombing of a village. But in Viet Nam that same veteran can be directly forgiven by the family that suffered the loss, thanked for returning, and accepted as a family member bringing back the soul of the lost loved one. And we can atone; we can rebuild what and where we have destroyed.

WE HAVE GIFTED TWO SCHOOLS where schools were destroyed and repaired others after typhoons. We have helped Agent Orange victims and centers, built homes for the disabled and an infirmary and bicycle garage for an orphanage, gifted water buffalo, pigs, chickens, and sampans to the neediest. In almost every case, veterans returning to Viet Nam achieve more healing and inner peace in two to three weeks of immersion in contemporary Viet Nam than they have achieved through conventional treatments and medications in their half-century at home since the war. The heart and soul need these encounters to be set aright with the painful past, the former foe now a friend, our own karmas, destinies, and life itself. As we prayed at a remote temple on the Perfume River, a local man instructed our group, "Help a fish in this lifetime and a fish will help you in the future." As we help the Vietnamese heal their land and infrastructure, they help heal our souls.

Beyond the Vietnamese and American veterans, there is a third voice in these poems. Some of them recount my experiences as I am touched, penetrated, and changed by these encounters. I began these journeys as urgent attempts to find the most comprehensive healing for American veterans. These evolved into experiences so deep and complex that I have become one with the Vietnamese as I have become one with our veterans. This needs expression and sharing through poetry.

POETRY IS THE LANGUAGE OF THE SOUL. Surrendering to its call we not only express our own deepest urges but also channel the experiences, images, feelings, motivations, voices, ideas, values, and visions of other peoples and cultures into our own. Poetry enables others' voices to sound through ours. It allows us to achieve a spiritual intimacy and cultural bridge with the other that transcend differences. Some of our most moving experiences in country have been shared poetry readings in which veterans' hearts and souls speak and survivors from each side grab the others' verses to exclaim, "Your story is my story. We are the same." The poems herein seek to express the soul of Viet Nam and of our warriors through the voices and experiences of Viet Nam's multitudes of honored women and men survivors and of our own who have had the courage to return to face and transform the wounds of the past. Poetry serves the causes of healing and promoting social justice, international understanding, and peace. This is "poetry of witness."

I gave a reading of some of these poems in Viet Nam's capital at a cultural celebration of Ha Noi's 995th anniversary. When I arrived at the event, the Writers Union representative said to me, "You Americans are so much a part of our history that we left an empty chair to represent you. We did not know an American writer would arrive, but please take the seat and read to us of what our country means to you."

After my reading an older woman approached me. She had survived the war but lost her children in a terrible way. She pointed to my poem, "Song of a Grieving Mother." She said, "How did you know? How is this possible? These were my feelings in your poem. You are an American man, but you give truthful voice to what we Vietnamese women sacrificed and suffered. Then indeed there is hope for healing between our countries and for our planet."

May it be so.

A NOTE ON LANGUAGE AND SPELLING: *Vietnamese is a mono-syllabic and tonal language. Every word is one syllable pronounced with a distinct tone. Vietnamese spelling is thus properly short one-syllable words. The country is Viet Nam, the capital Ha Noi, its largest city Sai Gon. Combining their names and words into complex Western words is another hidden form of cultural appropriation. Herein, to the degree comfortable and possible for English language readers, we return proper Vietnamese spelling to communicate respect and restore integrity.*

INVOCATIONS

1

LEAVING

*Long Quan is the name of the Dragon
who is the traditional mythological father
of the Vietnamese people, the only people
on the planet tracing their lineage directly
to Dragon Father.*

With the south-bound geese
I honk a sad farewell
to my fading home.

Amidst flapping wings
I am carried by hard steel
to meet the Dragon.

Each time, I carry
the sword of our wounds
to seek its return.

With a brother's heart
I guide our shattered warriors
between ox carts and memories.

With a father's heart
the Dragon's wings embrace us;
his fires cleanse; his waters soothe.

As geese find warm homes
let our griefs and ghosts be
welcomed by Dragon.

PRAYING

Never in my life did I pray so hard
as that day at the smoking bottom of this mountain,
among giant boulders and fallen trees,
when the enemy overran our wire
and sprouted like berserk rice stalks
no farther away than the length of my rifle
and our muzzle holes became God's wrathful eyes.

Never in my life did I pray so hard,
until today, on the cloud-crowned top of this mountain,
among smiling statues and wafting incense
when their children took my hands and called me Uncle
and monks bowed to me as if I were a saint
and I embraced their dead as my true brothers
and God's loving eyes gazed through my torn and
    mending heart.

SONG OF THE VIETNAMESE WOMEN

I will grow my rice beside your craters.
I will place my body before your tanks.
I will give my hands to stop your helicopters
and give my legs to cut your wire.
I will mark your minefields to protect my village
and hoe all day to stand watch all night.
I will dig and chop and lash and haul
to open jungle trails to foil you.

I will go without rice so our fighters may eat
and sing in the foxholes beneath your burning rain.
I will wrap myself in chains to show what you do
and bandage your wounds when you fall into my arms.
I will give my father, my husband, my sons,
and bless their leaving though I never see them again.
I will pray you return to your mothers' arms
and forgive you though you take everything I have.

I will feed my men whose hands you have shorn.
I will carry my sisters through the bleeding night.
I will tend my buffalo as your bombs fall down
and rebuild my dykes after you have blown them.
I will aim my plow as straight as my gun
and plant young rice and forge new bullets.
Long after you are gone and have forgotten me,
I will give my limbs to defuse your mines.

Made for feeding, caressing, sowing,
made for nursing, carrying, caring,
made for planting, harvesting, cooking,

made for threading, weaving, sewing,
made for singing, dancing, laughing,
made for acting, playing, loving,
come here with hatred and I will don
the helmet, the scope, the rifle, the bomb.

I am grandmother, mother, wife, daughter.
Make me angry and you cannot be right.
Make me mad and you cannot be just.
Make me rebel though all I am
wishes to birth and plant and grow;
make me resist and you show your heart.
Make me fight and you cannot win.
Make me stand and you will fall.
Return in peace and show me your wounds,
and I will bind them with love and call you brother.

Ancestors

For Nguyen Thi Que Mai

My grandfather's dust sprouts marble chips.
Rice grows in the field where your grandmother lies buried.
My grandfather's bones wear skyscraper shadows.
Your grandmother's bones sow new green stalks.
Remembrance stones crown my grandfather's headstone.
Cranes tickle your grandmother's skull.
I sway alone before the rock of grandfather's grave.
Your family feeds grandmother rice cakes.
My grandfather's stories wallpaper tenement halls.
Grandmother sings to you in every grain of rice.

2

VE: The Return

In this hot, wet, green world
I return to wander amidst
time-carved mountains, wind-sculpted pagodas,
and countless faces whose wrinkles seem
carved by gods into masks of toil and joy.
These have been my beacons and prayer towers
calling me again and again
to strain my legs and lungs,
to climb as high as I can,
to seek what lies beyond this blazing sky
and beneath our crinkled skin.

This year my wandering will be
on the heights and at the base of these mountains,
perhaps to glimpse on a breeze, in a fishpond,
in a child's black eyes or elder's smile,
in a stray and humble wildflower,
what all my striving could never see.

LAST DAY OF THE WAR
Tran Dinh Song, southern air force, April 30, 1975

In my uniform
of the defeated south,
no money, family, unit; cause all gone;
I watch tanks crash through the palace gates
and no longer know who I am.

*

The old gates crash,
the new flag flies.
I shed and shred
my uniform shirt
and disappear in the stampede.

*

Walking for days
through crowds of thousands
without food, clothing, hope,
carrying a lollipop sign,
"Brother, do you live?"

Rush Hour

2002

Like light straining to pierce an oldster's cataracts
the white fireball of morning greets me
through a hazy sky. It is my third year
of days begun on this simple span of concrete
arching across the gray-green Sai Gon River.
The small of my sagging back
is supported by the same span that upholds
these thousands. Here I stand, white and alone,
in a sea of flowing tan droplets,
in a torrent of falling yellow rain,
on a face flooded with ochre tears.
They stare. They nod. They grin.
Their eyes speak questions, dances, blessings.
It is for me to come, year after year,
to stand and greet through their rush hour.
It is for me to carry new things, things that smile,
to this place where we cargoed endless tears.
It is for me, on this teeming morning bridge,
to join the sun in burning off
the nightmares, the cataracts, the old fears
that keep me alone, that prevent us from becoming
a single sea, a single sky, a single face.

FIFTY YEARS AFTER THE WAR
2019

Over many years and visits I rose
as the great white pearl of sun climbed
its eastern ladder to scatter silvered drops
of light on the river and its thousands
of worker ants migrating on foot or bicycle
to their daily stations of labor or learning.

Now the pearl's drops bounce off skyscraper
windows whose lights diminish the sky.
Mopeds and gleaming cars have replaced sandals.
Racks of diamonds, clothing, Western wares
crowd the streets thick with names, faces and foods
stampeding here from everywhere on the globe.

Now at dawn I lie awake in bed,
aching for the lost hours when my Western face
was new and brave to be here
and I came only to escort the wounded souls
who fought here and embrace
the loving souls arrayed against them.

It was a divine limbo
when our inner poverty and their outer hunger
were the twins born of war
that threw us toward each other
as long-lost aching lovers
who had together given this strange birth.

Now I dig and dig through
the blasting lights of Gucci and Starbucks
that drown the early sun and aching hearts
to find those moments of pure connection
born of necessity of that other fire
that once fell screaming from this same sky.

LETTER TO NGUYEN CAO KY*

In Memory of Capt. Terry Bell

Sir,
the battle I fought for you,
the men I lost for you,
the men I killed for you,
and the death I lived for you
are no more.
You were doing your job,
I was doing mine,
and neither of us could know
we were hired by the wrong bosses
to do the work that should never be done.
Our work together,
meant to bring victory,
instead led to Tet
and lifetimes of losses.

But today,
before your empty throne
in this museum that was your palace,
my heart reopens its doors
locked long ago for you.
I address your wandering spirit
and declare that, for my men and my soul,
I shall live.

*Ky, a military officer and politician, was chief of the Republic of
Vietnam Air Force in the 1960s, then in a military junta South Viet
Nam's prime minister from 1965 to 1967. He personally awarded
Capt. Bell a medal.*

With this final salute
I cleanse my chest of your touch
and declare myself free of malice.
I leave you here
to return to myself.
Now I am free to walk.

With sincere regards,
TB

TUYEN
13-year-old street vendor

Crying our wares
in the midnight shadows –
the painted woman and me

Selling postcards –
the way I grow rice
for my family

Don't be offended
by the whore's anger –
she too must eat

Your people come
for war, shopping, movies –
I am always here

Why is street life
so hard? not enough time
to read

Who dares say
that noon is more beautiful
than midnight?

CHUNG
Singer, Agent Orange Victims Band

This year I walk on three legs.
Your legs are stumps and you cannot stand.
My ears never stop ringing.
You cannot hear.
My eyes are cloudy and squinting.
Your face is smooth and empty where eyes should be.
I cannot speak your language.
You have none.
Yet your voice, your song, the wind that blows through you
resounds from your tiny, twisted body,
a great bronze prayer bell
peeling dawn into our darkened world.

MASSAGE GIRL

24-year-old Linh from the southern countryside

First of five daughters—
my parents plant young rice sprouts
I knead your muscles

Fourteen hours a day
my father plants, sows, harvests
I soothe weary feet

My father's rice paddies
thick with green shoots
and rusting shrapnel

Among sputtering mopeds
how I miss
our plodding buffalo

One day each month—
my only holiday—
the long ride home

$20 monthly wage
for my room, clothes, food—
tips to carry home

My mother
land, sisters, ancestors—
tears on my pillow

My father and you—
sixty-year-old same-same—
how are you so young?

My brown skin—
the flag of the weary poor—
will you make a trade?

My story—
your smile—
happiness

Cyclo Driver

Nam, middle-aged orphaned son of a Southern Air Force pilot

Colonel my father
long sword hanging from his belt—
men and I salute

Zip zip through the sky
leading steel birds of flame—
I play in the dirt

VC bang bang
tearing apart his plane
and my heart

My mother wailing—
I must walk tall
carrying his bones

Hat, shoulder bars, sword—
my mother's memory chest
in our far village

Peddling all day—
I don't march, I don't plow—
thighs ache and ache

I listen—
revolutionary songs—
I don't sing

From its ashes
my phoenix
does not rise

At the Fine Arts Museum

"Thunderstorm"

Our horses panic –
their limbs and ours flee the wind –
the rice grass just bows

"House on Stilts"

The palms' reflections
as perfect as the trees above
in the still still lake

"Uncle Ho Goes Fishing"

Fishing alone
in blue-green mountain waters –
my independence

"Beside the Row of Bamboo Trees"

Is it clouds, cotton,
or tufts of snared fairy hair
caught in the bamboo webs
lining the blue river?

Three Poems from the Forest of Enlightenment

1
In the Garden
Before a great Buddha statue

Sweet sutras dripping from her tongue
she sits before Buddha cross-legged and sincere
while traffic squeals and children squawk.
I light my joss stick and take my place
beside her supine form. Only then,
in this small banyan park, do I see
the raw flesh stretched thin, the crooked scar
that crawls from where her ear should be
to plunge beneath her plain and simple dress.
I strain to keep my gaze on Buddha.
She just bows and sings.
I kowtow with my glowing sticks
less to the calm Lord in marble
than to this woman with the wounds of the world
fried into her living flesh.

2

IN THE PAGODA

Praying with Buddha—
burning fires in my sore heart
soothed by cooling rain

Two child-monks chanting
between bells and deep drumbeats
the yapping puppy

The smiling boy-monk
pounding his heavy drumsticks
on the skin of my heart

In this sour chanting
what dies and what is born?
Only me again

In Meditation

How can I grow your lotus
so that it blooms in my heart?

Live your life like an arrow
sure it will hit its mark.

How can I grow your lotus
so that it blooms in my heart?

What passes is illusion.
Tend what endures.

3

Long-Haired Warrior

Ngo Thanh Thuy is a Viet Cong veteran, a "long-haired warrior" as the women fighters were called. She enlisted in the Viet Cong at ten-years-old after her school was destroyed by American warplanes.

> Amidst dead children
> I follow my teacher
> into battle.

Serving as a courier she met her future husband, Lam Van Tien, who became a Viet Cong unit commander while fighting the war. Unlike American GIs, Vietnamese troops were in the war until it was over or they were wounded or killed. Their company commander married them in a simple jungle ceremony.

> I speak my vows
> to my man and country—
> honeymoon ambush.

The couple began their family during the war. While fighting and struggling, they had three children. One severely disabled from Agent Orange died within days of birth.

> Nursing babies—
> fighting invaders—
> war inside and out.

Tam Tien was severely wounded twice. With a joyous
laugh he lifts his shirt to show his scars. This family
began a farm on war-decimated land granted by the
government to veterans. On this island across the river
from Vinh Long they live with their families in a restored
green paradise they have labored since the war to rebuild.

> Dragon eyes, mangoes, eels, snails,
> turtles, grandchildren—
> tides in, out, in.

Now they offer tea, pineapples, and red spiked *chum
chums*. Tonight elephant ear fish and giant prawns. They
joke and smile with this group of American visitors. They
are especially anxious to hear American vets' stories and
offer their hospitality.

> Last time you must leave.
> But tonight please dream
> on my pillow.

DELTA DAWN

From horizon to horizon
this sky is a single sheet of gray.
The palms are upright black sentinels
standing tall and reaching crinkled limbs
against this drab pre-dawn sheet.
The edges of the thatched roof over my head
are black fingers and thorns scratching the gray.

Below the torn hammock cradling my insomnia
the floodwaters spread a wet blanket
over the supping earth, reflecting
in this haze the same gray-black canopy above.
Is the sky above and earth below?
Is the water above and sky below?
I am the filling of this sandwich.

All I know here, swinging in this space
to the tune of constant cackling roosters
and early buzzing cicadas,
all I know is the smile in my heart
to be blessed with sleeplessness
so that I can learn to swing in the void
and finally know it
as a great and warm and wet embrace.

SWIMMING

Evening

I swim through the humid air
in a swarm of red dragonflies.
The white crescent moon above
is grandmother's distant smile.

Morning

Shimmering sunbeams
through parting gray mist and clouds,
tepid green waters,
thick hyacinth clumps, fin splash –
I dive into breaking dawn.

HYACINTHS

Did I not see you,
green hyacinth clump,
tugging your baby shoots
and trading your bearded roots
as you floated to the sea
under the blazing midday sun?
You return now, a black silhouette,
a thief in the night,
floating upriver to the place of your birth.
The journey ends where it began.
The journey begins at its end.
You and I are the single breath
sucked in, sucked out, in, out.
We are the breath of the sea.

Delta Haiku

Travelling

I left my god-fruit*
in the hotel refrigerator
blessing the ice cubes

Dawn

Giant plop and splash
off the wooden bridge's rim—
first morning greeting

Boatwoman

Tangled hyacinths
cling to her long wooden oars—
she tugs, glides, sighs, tugs

Landscape

Palm fronds bouncing—
banana leaves bowing—
star bull blazing

*God-fruit had been placed as offerings on ancestor altars, consid-
ered especially blessed and healthy and sometimes later gifted or
consumed.*

Floating Market
Ca Be Village

In the muddy wake
of the brimming cabbage boat
two floating sandals

Farming

Tending my paddy
my neighbor's bending back
aches as much as mine

Incense

Nine burning sticks—
three times three, three times the luck
simply to pray

Sleepless

Counting sheep, breaths, cocks' crows, oms—
all I do is count, count, count
while the thin moon wanes

Moth

Iridescence
streaking across the black sky –
star shooting to Earth

Duty
Nghiep, student recruiter, Cambodian War veteran

Behind the dirt dyke
the crumbling martyr's bunker—
my grandfather's grave

On holy days I feast both
ancestors and wanderers

RECONCILIATIONS

The Toast

Drink my hot bullets,
I said in the dark jungle;
drink my wine today

Body Bag

In your body bag
taken then returned by you
my soldier son's bones

POINT OF VIEW

A weary Marine asked Nguyen Tam Ho, "Mr. Tiger,"
a veteran of 25 years of combat against three invading
nations, why he did not suffer survivor's guilt as do
Americans. "I am sad but not guilty," he answered. "
Perhaps the bullet is the messenger of karma. Learn
to see our lives from the point of view of the bullet."

From the point of view of the bullet
one will live, one will die.

From the point of view of a man
my life is his death.

From the point of view of the bullet
you took the right step, he the wrong.

From the point of view of a man
his death should have been mine.

From the point of view of the bullet
fate is a swift straight shot.

From the point of view of a man
fate is a fickle whore.

From the point of view of the bullet
I am a servant of destiny.

From the point of view of a man
destiny is a greedy whore.

From the point of view of the bullet
his destiny was complete.

From the point of view of a man
he left me to live for two.

From the point of view of the bullet
you survived to finish your mission.

From the point of view of a man
I wish I had died instead.

From the point of view of the bullet
your service was not your mission.

From the point of view of a man
my time in hell was enough.

From the point of view of the bullet
life wants more from you.

From the point of view of a man
tell me what I must do.

From the point of view of the bullet
live for all who died.

From the point of view of a man
too many lamenting ghosts.

From the point of view of the bullet
those voices are now your voice.

From the point of view of a man
those voices are now my voice.

RECOVERING RONNIE

Seeking a GI's death site

His fishing line falls
into murky green waters—
my old ambush bridge

Among the thick leaves
buffalo, farms and old tombs—
Where did we live and die?

How could I know
it was this littered mud lane—
the smiling Buddha

Rows of wet paddies
covering my old firebase—
bittermelon vines

The young farmer
pointing to grandfather's fields—
your tanks, our melons

Sobbing sad taps
into my old harmonica—
distant sutra chants

Half a century
to bring his soul home—
shrapnel in my heart

Shrapnel and sorrow—
Viet Nam in my body—
We are always one

She wraps small brown arms
around my heavy white frame—
"We love you!"

Fifty years
for this one moment
together again

BOAT'S EYES

May the red eye on the bow of my boat
stare without flinching
into the glaring eye of the monster
that rises from the murky bottom
of this long river that is our home.

May I return with baskets full
with this load of fish
to feed my hungry family
and for one more day
escape being food for the monster.

FISH MARKET
Vinh Long

One looks like a pair of lungs
beating and breathing without a body.
The next sprouts a leg and toes
its entire snakelike length.
Its neighbor is a crab pinching air.
Beside it turtles beat small legs
in a panic against their basin.

A catfish heaves its strong sleek body
out of its pan of shallow water.
It squeezes, contracts, stretches, beats
its gray and slimy length up the baked mud street.
I pray it reaches the river, but halfway up the street
between round *long ans*, spiked *chum chums*,*
knives, cleavers, bags of new green tea,
its ragged racing vendor grabs it by the tail.
His neighbors point and laugh
as he returns it squirming in his fist
to its shallow pain whose flowing river
is a thin black hose keeping it alive
and fresh until another fist will carry it
to a nearby hut for dinner.

These, these, all these thousands –
desperate gills sucking air
as they squirm on their backs and sides –
these perform their last dance,
their dance of death,
so that we who walk may live.

Long ans and chum chums – regional traditional fruits

Booby Traps

The GI

My flesh and my blood
torn by your tripwire grenade –
me here forever

The VC

Hanging beehives
released to attack you before –
share my honey now

Together

On silt-green waters
our old and secret stories
drip from smiling lips

NHAC SANH*

I walk through a darkness
as thick and wet as hot black soup.
Distant riverboats sputter. Distant stars prickle.
Out of this liquid midnight
a dog stirs, yaps three times as I pass,
then fades back into shadows.

In our bunkhouse old vets sleep.
Nhac Sanh's song once told them
no enemy was near. All is silent save for their snores
and the constant song of our single tree locust
screeching, screeching, screeching,
prying the rusty hinges of our hearts
open again on this invisible, eternal river.
Tonight they are safe to dream.

*A night-singing cicada-family insect the size and shape of a
large locust.

JUNGLE NIGHT

I walk in the mud to the edge of darkness
and stop where it cannot be pierced.
Chameleons click. Crickets chirp.
Moth wings flutter like silken cymbals.
When we are born, sound comes first.
When we die, sound leaves last.
Here where the entire universe seems
a tunnel of infinite black,
I see nothing, know nothing,
realize I am nothing
but a breath suspended
between the birth and death and rebirth
of all that was and is and will be.

VIET CONG STRONGHOLD
For Tam Tien and his family

1
For hours I watch
and struggle to decipher
the yellow letters
inscribed on the jungle night
by the swirling comet's tail
of the single firefly trapped
inside the old nurse's mosquito net
in the bunk next to mine.

2
Crickets, chameleons,
bat wings, and sputtering boats
keep my ears from sleeping.
I listen through the black night
while in the next bunk
undisturbed by ghosts
the graying grunt snores.

3
Ripples lap my muddy toes
behind the hedge of water hyacinth
lining this tiny inlet—
one among thousands—
of the old Viet Cong couple
who pointed to their scars,

fried us fresh catfish
on burning straw,
and laughed as we devoured
their love.

4
In the blackness
I climb into their hammock,
suspended between *long an* trees,
dog yelps and rooster calls.
My head snuggles and sways
on the thick green linen,
but my long white legs
dangle over the sides
and tumble toward the muddy river.
I prop my heels
in tangled vines
as my mind untangles from war.

5
After my hosts
fish and bathe in the brown waters,
after their green tea
steams in old, cracked pots,
before my Americans open their weary eyes,
geckos scurry along the twisting branches
inches from my nose
and the first light of dawn
slithers through the cracking horizon
as the cosmic egg hatches us
for one more day.

6

As the gray light spreads
and the river ripples in purple and pink,
the old guerilla, bushy brows sprouting gray,
joins me carrying a white teapot
painted with two red roses.
He hands us each a cup.
We toast and laugh and talk
until we run out of each other's words.
Then, so we can converse,
he takes out his mandolin
and, just for me, he sings.

ANOTHER DELTA DAWN

The morning star is a single shining eye
above the grinning mouth of the crescent moon.
A rooster crows. Shivers wriggle down my spine.
In the green waters lapping at my feet,
an unseen mouth rises and gulps,
sinks and gulps again. Birds whistle.
Their winged silhouettes streak the blue sky.
Early boats sputter and cross.
Fishermen pole their rafts and toss their nets.
The sun's first rays drape the horizon.
A line of light clouds drape dawn's bridal veil.
Our host's strong laughter rises
with the first sunrays and his steaming tea.
Peel the veil. Kiss the day.
Drink his laughter. Chirp and caw.
Here we cannot be alone
and all we are
rises with the fireball.

MEKONG REBIRTH

1
Today the rising fireball
is softened by a cloak of gray clouds.
It stares as it rises
above the crinkled horizon—
a god's eye coated in cataracts.
The silhouettes of branches crisscross
as dark veins feeding the firmament.
Here where only burnt sticks, mud, and ash
remained from my country's first visit
with the fire that rains and fries, I am surrounded
by thick green banana, palm, guava, and jackfruit trees
and finally, finally the birds have returned
to sing and dance on these ancient new limbs.

2
Flashes of indigo in *long an* trees,
upright storks in hyacinth clumps,
swift black arrows of ducks sandwiched
between gray sky and silt-brown river,
whistles, clacks, caws at dawn and dusk—
into this green wet world
silenced for half a century
the birds, the birds, the birds have returned.

FLOWERS BLOOMING INSIDE THE ENEMY
For Tam Tien

Once you were the flower
that blossomed on my base.
Your petals spit fire.
Your leaves blazed hate.
Your spider-webbed face
taught me how to fear.

Today you are the flower
that blossoms on this river.
Your petals drip kindness.
Your leaves caress mine.
My lost years fade to nothing
as you teach me again to love.

HANG NGA AT DAWN

*Hang Nga, goddess of the moon, combines
the attributes of the western deities Artemis,
guardian of maidens and wild creatures,
and Aphrodite, goddess of love and beauty.*

Even as the thin low clouds
floating above the eastern horizon
stain pink and burn from the unseen sun,
the crescent moon is the smile of a goddess
looking down from her cobalt porch
on these silvered waters and stretching dogs.
Roosters cry from four directions.
Palm fronds frolic on a soft breeze.
Thick and torn leaves flutter like prayer flags,
sending their greetings from this hard mud
back up to her smile that does not fade.
Pinpoint stars are her freckles and dimples,
but her nose, eyes, brow, and hair
are blue and hidden behind the veil of the sky.

The pink spreads. The horizon lightens.
Dogs yawn, stretch, and rise to wander.
Boat motors clack and groan. Water boils.
My neighbors' teakettles steam and sing.
Hyacinth clumps skid toward the distant sea.
Throats and radios sound the voices of dawn
that crackle and mingle with the motors' sputter.

Now the clouds burn. Her freckles disappear.
A last white dimple clings to the corner of her grin,
then it too is swallowed by the spreading blue.
The silhouettes of birds show
pink and blue through stretching feathers.
Long necks tow them on their morning search.

Now her veil is blue. Now the pink clouds
cloak her shoulders. Now the steaming kettles
are tipped. Black leaves turn green. People stretch
and wander with the dogs. More motors.
More boats. More dogs. More cooking.
Black night folds like a threadbare blanket.

White light spreads. The moon goddess draws
the veil of the dawn across her face. All disappears
except her white smile that remains on high
to grace us through this Delta day.

TAY NINH PROVINCE

THE IRON TRIANGLE

4

MINH'S HOUSE

The footfalls of the world
tramp the mud in my front yard
and walk past my small altar to our land god.
People smile. They say *xin chao.*
They even stop to shake my hand.
But you ask my name, my age,
my family, and—more precious than rice—
you ask of the graves beside my home.
I only have this small bit of land.
It does not matter. My wife, my mother, and hers,
my grand mum, all sleep side by side.
Those who were and those yet to be
are one in us and through us.
You light my incense,
bow and pray to spirits of those you never knew.
You are the first. You are kind.
You lift the sorrow from my heart
and gift me this lucky day.
In the smoke of incense and the rising prayers
you and I are also one.

CONVERSATION IN THE JUNGLE

for Tran Dinh Song

"Look at your earth's torn flesh,
these deep pits and scars,
trees like bloody stumps of arms
held high in surrender.
I stare at this green emptiness
and offer you my endless grief."

"Look at this earthen well
hugging green rainwater.
Look at the carpet of bamboo
sprouting from our earth's deep flesh.
Cleanse this cloud of grief from your eyes
and see."

At Cu Chi

In the dank tunnel
our nurse leans her crutches
on their operating table

AT KIM PHUC'S HOUSE

*Kim Phuc was the 9-year-old girl in the
world-famous 1972 photograph shown napalmed
and fleeing. She is now an international peace
activist living in Canada.*

Trang Bang

Here they farmed
here they married
here they parented
here they grew

Here we came
here we bombed
here they fled
here they burned

Here they cried
here they grieved
here she left
here he stayed

Here he married
here he fathered
here we came
here we met

Here we shared
here we cried
here he laughed
here we hugged

Here they grew
here he died
here we came
and here we are

BROTHER TAM

Kim's brother Phan Thanh Tam,
caught in the same bombing, lost an eye.
Until his death he remained in their
family home and hosted us during visits.

Left eye
seared blind by napalm
above his toothless grin

Beneath the framed photo
of fleeing scorched children
we sip his coffee

WHERE FIRE RAINED

In Memory of Jim Helt, US Air Force, Bien Hoa Air Base

Before the blue and yellow temple
where fire rained on children
from the steel birds he once helped steer,
the gray-grizzled vet plants his sandals
in the shadowy footprints
of the fleeing frying girl.
He shuts his eyelids tight
to take leave of sunlight, bicycles, and buffalo.
In his darkness he sees red,
only red, everywhere bright, hot red.
The elements, too, have souls.
He answers the ghost of fire
in the only way he can.
He bows his head and prays.

AT VIET CONG HEADQUARTERS
Xa Mat Tan Bien, near the Cambodian border

Tunnels, trenches, huts
empty now.
Benches, wells, paths
long unused.
Trees, vines, centipedes
silent, safe.
Bomb craters
deep, green, sprouting.

I descend stone steps,
crawl down a dark corridor,
startle a black bat that startles me.
No one here
but unseen chattering monkeys
and silent wandering ghosts.
A whisper in my ear,
"This is a memorial highway."

THE BAT

I stand in the dank shade of banyans and palms
and peer into the hole at my feet.
Here the soldiers, here their command
fled from the fire dropped from the sky
and its thunder that convulsed the earth.
Here they huddled. Here they hid.
Here they clung to each other and the walls
more fiercely than the roots that knit this earth.

I descend the first step, the second, the third,
on the moss-covered stones into earth's belly.
The walls drip with slime, the torpid air thickens.
The light fades to ash, then to gray, then to black.
Above all was ash though now it is green.
Below all black. The darkness remains.
My feet hit bottom. I crouch and crawl,
sensing old breathing, old terror, old rage.

I crawl where they crawled. I tremble. I sweat.
Slight light from the hole above guides my way.
My country once threw "Fire in the hole!"
Now I am the only American flame.
Deep into darkness that once saved or killed,
I stare, I peer, I ask who is there.
No mortal answer, no human stink,
only stillness and my beating heart.
Then without warning, a rustle, a shudder,
a black bat swoops toward me with outstretched wings.

A mask on my eyes, a slap on my face,
its swift wings buzz and fan me awake.
A bat in this tunnel, a bat in its home;
a bat swooping in peacetime has long been a sign.
My terror subsides. I step and chuckle.
My grimace melts to a sigh and a smile.
Long life and riches, goodness and health—
here bats are omens that carry these gifts.

Now only bats dwell here. Now I must leave
to let them all live as I crawl toward good death.

ATOP LADY BLACK MOUNTAIN
In the Nui Ba Den Pagoda

Remembering
his bloody ascent—
a lone bird sings

Grieving
those who fell on these boulders –
a cool breeze blows

Praying
for wandering souls –
a waterfall gurgles

Cross-legged
amidst chanting monks –
a baby giggles

Descending
in drizzle and lightening –
tree frogs croak

5

DA NANG

*At the Quan Am Pagoda ***
The Mountain of Water, Marble Mountain

His thousand-yard stare
staring into
the monk's clear eyes

Water droplets—
sweet sutras pouring
from the goddess's vessel

The old vet bows—
dropping from the sky
the monk's prayer beads

The monk's smiling eyes
caressing and melting
his thousand-yard stare

**Quan Am is the Vietnamese goddess of mercy, known more
commonly by the Chinese name Quan Yin. She is also called Lady
Buddha and her statue stands outside most Vietnamese pagodas.*

CHILDHOOD MEMORY

Tran Dinh Song

I loved the stars so much
I could not sleep indoors.
but mother made me take to bed
despite my lonely tears.
Brother dried them and released a jar
of fireflies beneath my mosquito netting.
I slept in a swirl of living stars.

STREET VENDOR
Hoa, an aging street woman

My name Hoa. Captain name me Suzy.
I grow rice. Captain teach me type.
I speak Viet. Captain teach me English.
I believe we friends. Captain leave me 45 year ago.
Captain go home. I homeless.
Now I sell juice on street.
This small wagon my shop.
I strain and strain to remember your words.
This first time I speak English since Captain.
I say we friends but he forget.
You come back. You buy juice. You talk me.
Maybe you not forget.

WINDY TOMB
For the extended family of Tran Dinh Song

Alive, our souls
need a house to be home.
Dead, our souls
need a tomb for deep rest.
Without a house
we are homeless.
Without a tomb
we wander without return.

My uncle was VC,
his son was ARVN—
North and South,
just like your war.
My uncle was buried
when your tank crushed his tunnel.
My cousin's bones sleep
in a mass grave for both sides.

My family searched
with shovels and spoons,
but we could not overturn
the earth and the water.
Finally, finally,
we built windy tombs—
tombs without bodies,
tombs without bones.

Finally, finally,
father and son
sleep together,

rest again.
Once every year
when the moon cries its tears *
with rice porridge and cookies
we join in sad feast.

*The Day of Wandering Souls, an annual autumn sacred day
to honor the MIAs, "wandering souls" whose bodies have never
been recovered.

Old Da Nang Base

China Beach footprints
washed away by time and tides
and hotel debris

Jungle clearing—
fallen trees, chopped bamboo,
scattered plastic chairs—
Drinking beer with VC troops—
now and then, then and now

No sandals, no eyes—
water bottle begging bowl—
dancing fingers flute song

My firebase barber—
noontime shave, haircut, ear cleaning—
midnight satchel bombs—
Today his razor on my throat
purifies us both for Tet

Graffiti scrawled
under the watchtower—
"God forgives"

MISCARRIAGE

For Huyen Thi Lan

I have one baby
but feel two pink mouths pulling
at my swollen breasts.

We build an altar
the size of toys and candy.
Now both babies rest.

A Mother's Tet Prayer

For Lan

I place fruit and candy on his altar,
light five incense sticks and kowtow three times,
burn paper clothes and a giant paper horse
so he can ride through our happy village.
As I greet him my smile is a needle
knitting together the patches of my heart.
In this way the child who was never born
enters our home to share our New Year's joy.

LEAVING DA NANG

This hot airport
where I killed and almost died –
just another airport.

Standing watch
over carry-on luggage
I salute and laugh.

For a half century I have been
a rucksack of aching wounds.
Today I am a pillow.

CHU LAI
*Site of the first major battle
against the Viet Cong, 1965*

CHU LAI RETURN
In Honor and Memory of Nupkus and Wil

My first night here
ordered to hold that spit of land—
my cherry breaks

Suicide attack—
stand and fight or duck and run—
both suicide

K-bar in my fist
I slice and slash and stab
only to save my brothers

I stoop and sprinkle tobacco
over his fallen body
but I cannot drink his blood

The smoke clears
Where are my brothers?
Where is my soul?

Loading their bodies
onto a dump truck,
their grave one big hole

My kindly guide—
his VC grandfather
by my hand in that hole

On the windy tomb
87 incense sticks—
my fallen brothers

Creator said,
"Do not kill." After four decades
my ears open.

RAIN IN THE FACE

Thick gray mist
clouding his vision
of his old hanger

Pelting raindrops
dribbling down the war monument
and the veteran's cheeks

"Who sheds blood with me..."
tumbling from the GI's lips
into green rice paddies

School holiday—
crouching beneath dripping trees
two children

The American War Nurse
Builds a Windy Tomb

For Beth Marie Murphy

My back is bowed from decades
of carrying the soul of the legless girl
who began as my patient then became my niece
as we flew colored kites in the wind off my ship.

In dreams my eyes are pink and swollen
with the ocean of tears both shed and withheld
since the angry wounded called her *VC child*
and desperate arms snatched her back to the jungle.

Today I carry one stone at a time.
With each dripping tear I recite her name.
Gently I let her down off my back
and give my lost niece this tomb for a home.

Eight children tumble around my fractured legs
to help me lay the last stones on her cairn.
A single red dragonfly hovers in our wafting incense
and a sweet breeze kisses my cheek with her name.

THE BEAR HUG

For Nupkus Roger Shourds, "Sees the Bear,"
Salish Warrior, US Marine

1

"It's true," grunted the old Marine
as his log-thick forearm circled my neck.
"Closer than a wife," he cooed
and yanked my head against his.
"Deeper than sex," and his free hand
rolled into the same grip that had grasped
the hilt of his honed K-bar blade
reversed and hidden against his forearm.
"How could I marry like this?"
and his hand whipped the air across my throat
with the same fierce caress of the invisible blade
along the soft, brown-skinned throats
of those he had hugged on these white
and blood-stained sands half a century ago.

2

He released my neck—
was it a grunt or a laugh?—
and we turned together
toward the coming of the *pho.**

*Pho – Vietnamese noodle soup, the traditional national dish

HOI AN

MIDNIGHT BY THE BON THON RIVER

Dull gray clouds hide the moon and stars.
Old women as small as children sell
paper-boat candles on the quay.
We cup them in our hands, then set them afloat.
We cannot know who will receive our prayers,
but the reflected flames on black waters
burn constellations onto the flooded street.

HOSPITALITY

Tui, 65-year-old woman water taxi operator

When Heaven spills on our paddies
or swells our river, we rejoice.
But the only water
in what you dropped on my childhood
dripped from my cheeks as I fled.

Now you sit on the rotting plank seat
of my puttering boat
as we cruise between these riverbanks together.
This time no one flees
and it is not my cheeks that drip.

REUNION

Son, a 40-year-old sculptor

It has been a hard year.
First my old grandfather, survivor
of floods, famines, and four wars, died.
Then my uncle, suddenly.
Finally my father fell ill.
For weeks I sat by his side in hospital
but by Tet he was gone.
His funeral took all the money we had.
I could not think. I could not work.
I could not feed my mother and brother.
And that is why, after September 11,
though I worried about you, I did not write.
I have examined my mistake.
Now I ask you, please, friend,
can you forgive me?

DOOR EYES

From above the wooden lintel
two chrysanthemum eyes
stare through painted petals
to spill a yin-yang perfume
on every passing soul.
On one side, dragon roars.
On the other, tiger claws.
As we cross their humble threshold
we are both safe and blessed.

TET

All that is left
of my graying hippie hair
on the barber's floor

Dragon rising
on this New Year evening—
my golden balloon

"The rocket's red glare,
the bombs bursting in air..."
only fireworks

Midnight fireworks –
louder and more colorful –
the monk's chanting

Morning mist rising
from the puddled sidewalks
steaming my wrinkled heart

Please visit my shop.
Don't buy. Let me brew you tea.
Tell me your stories.
We will talk and talk and talk.
Friendship is the truest wealth.

MOTHER AND DAUGHTER
For Kate

She returned on Tet
and cloaked my heart with sun.
When I bowed before the altar
I felt her bowing in return.
But then a chilling wind
blew in thick clouds and rain.
The sky turned gray. My heart went blue.
The fireworks and chanting around us
ran like droplets off my cloak.
We walked the alleys arm in arm
and I was a babe in her bed.
My sleep was deep, long, and sad
as if we sat and talked together
before an invisible empty tomb.
Now, today, the third Tet dawn,
families bid ancestors farewell,
early sun breaks open the clouds,
light and heat dry my secret tears.
I rise like a kite as high as I can stretch
and smile again in certainty
that she is by my side.

MY LAI

Site of the March 16, 1968 massacre

MY LAI GUIDE I

Huyen, middle aged niece of massacre victims

Kettle, flame, scattered straw.
Dawn breaks. My great aunt cooks rice.
Her three children play and hug her legs.

Kettle dumped, flames galloping through straw.
Dawn burns. My aunt's face twists.
Three days before she had given them rice.

Their last moment before your people
landed in the paddies behind her hut –
their last hour as your people
taunted them beside the ditch.
These two moments are photographs
I can neither blend nor dissolve.

I left for college.
I left to learn your language.
I left to burn these photos.
But I want to die here too.
Until I do, I will tell the story.
Their last moment must last forever.

MY LAI GUIDE II
Kim, mid 30s

My husband and I try and try,
but each time we plant a child
it rushes away from my womb
to join my ancestors.

My doctor scolds—
too much talk about the war.
But my grandmother, my aunt,
my elder cousins all died here.

Tears for my ancestors,
tears for my children,
tears for the ghosts made of both.
Light incense with me.

THE GARDENER

Sapa, a 90-year-old massacre survivor

Bright-eyed boy
playing peek-a-boo
on my mother's grave

Beyond the ditch
where my daughters died –
new green rice

Each snip
of my rusty scissors
a gun blast

You wish to help me heal?
please let me
forgive you

HUE

RETURN TO PHU BAI

Forty years and half the globe
to return to see
an empty field,
an unused airstrip,
a green plain with no hooches
chewing water buffalo and sprouting weeds.

The tears I shed here today
have been leaking for decades
from my broken heart at home,
but they melt my mouth into a smile
that I have not felt or worn
since I was a boy and did not know war.

DAWN

I lie in darkness. My breathing is heavy and I cannot sleep.
Beside me my wife's breath slices the humid air
like a knife through a sponge.
From the nearby Citadel I hear the sighs
of ghosts that wander bleeding and without shoes.
On the river outside my window the dragon-headed boats
snuggle into the waters as in sheets without ripples
and wait to carry us to the nearby pagoda
where the inhalations of the monks already at prayer
cross-legged before the Maiden of Mercy
tug the first slivers of dawn toward our chins.

At the Hon Chen Temple

On the Perfume River. In Memory of George S.

I stand before the stone altar
of this goddess older than time,
on slick floor tiles, under dripping eaves,
where waters, stones, pillars, and wood
are all green. I breathe green.
I bow and call, kowtow and cry.
My wafting incense fumes inscribe his name.

*Po Nagar** guards the souls
of those who have gone beyond.
Her nostrils drink our incense.
She accepts our fruit and prayers
and eats our tears as heart-food.
She hears our losses. She calls him to us.
In her gaze we many are forever One.

*Ancient Cham name of the Taoist goddess worshipped at this
temple who determined the connections of souls after death.*

THE CENTRAL HIGHLANDS

QUANG TRI PROVINCE

6

In the Holy Wind Pagoda

The crumbling stupa—
sitting beside dead nuns' dust,
ants climbing my thighs

We hold living hands
in remembrance of our dead—
a sweet breeze answers

Fruit like giant tears
in tangled jackfruit trees—
tears on my cheeks

Rice cakes and incense—
the old nun insists we eat,
her novice laughs

Discerning the names
of our lost loved ones
inside their droning chants

The sad old vet
praying for those he killed
amid smiling nuns

The elder nun's farewell—
we all seek the same
peace, peace, peace

Mountain Guide

Le, 40-year-old regional tour guide

"Learn their language and be their guide,"
my father said as he grasped the wheel
and I bounced beside him in the green jeep
along poisoned and bomb-pocked roads
while the white giant in the steel hat
ruffled my hair from behind
then dropped sweet candy into my lap
like a gift from the emperor of the sky.
And so I did. And now,
in my own country, in my green home,
so I am.

In the Market

Grandmother stoops on skeletal legs
as crooked as those of the crabs
she grabs with knotty fingers.
They scrape and scamper.
Though as twisted, she is faster.
One by one she holds them
between left thumb and middle finger.
With her right hand she grabs
rusty scissors. She snips off
their bony legs one by one.
She tosses each stumpy crab
into a pile. They wriggle
but cannot move. She scoops them
into a plastic bag and plunks it
on her ancient scale
then hands it to her customer
for a few thousand *dong.* *
The shopper whisks off with her wriggling bag.
Grandmother remains behind
stooping on her twisted legs
unmoving among the scores of crab's legs
and the remaining wriggling shells.

*Dong is the basic unit of Vietnamese currency. Currently, roughly
23,000 dong = $1 US.*

At the Windy Tomb

Our incense smoke wraps the old stone monument
as if it were climbing a spiral staircase to the heavens.
We are taught that the souls of those who fell here
will wail and wander until they smell our smoke.
On this gray rock, under this blue sky,
we burn away our grief as we call their names.
Dragonflies and butterflies carpet our footsteps.
From a great distance a lone trumpet sounds.

AGENT ORANGE AFTERMATH

Van, middle-aged woman

Though I have two grown children,
I have never heard
that single word that drips
like honey on the heart,
"Mother."

Massage Girl – II

Tram, 35, from the mountains

My mother is dead,
all my brothers and sisters married.
I have no husband,
no education,
no other work.
I do not care that you are married.
I too hope to marry someday.
I will not tell anyone.
But with wars, SARS, chicken flu,
there are few tourists now.
I have no customers for two days,
while my old father,
alone in our mountain village,
is hungry and ill.
That is why I offer
to suck or fuck you.
The price you pay
will feed him for two weeks.
Please, sir, do not refuse.
What else can I do?

RETURN TO DRAGON MOUNTAIN
A huge old American military base outside Pleiku

Beneath red clay
grasping roots,
buried mines

Stooping in tall grass
I pick up the old release
expecting to die

I twirl green plastic
between my fingers
feeling nothing

No blast, no shrapnel –
a black butterfly –
breakfast explodes

Bad soup morning—
medicine
for my poisoned past

This mine pressure plate
I planted decades ago
opens my guts today

Khe Sanh

Memory

The chaplain dives in—
communion in the bunker—
Heaven burns above

Today

Our old dog tags
hanging behind the glass
in their museum

Four husky airmen
sweeping the ground of Khe Sanh
on leave from Iraq

Burned rotting tank hull—
sprouting through its turret holes
eucalyptus trees

THE ROAD TO DAK TO

Buddhists and Christians—
separate graveyards then—
sleeping together now

Burning incense
atop the eye sockets
of those who died here

Singed hills, charred trees,
his grin that does not feel—
only old photos

Bouncing on the bus
our middle-aged bellies
his dripping tears

Our smiling guide
born as our chaplain signed the cross
over empty boots

Tree stumps, shell holes—
water buffalo plod
beneath rubber trees

Where I raced my jeep
to dodge sniper rounds
four girls on a scooter

A million bomb craters—
cashew plantations,
fishing ponds

All green now
the old vet only recognizes
mountains and rain

Behind every tree
I feared who I would meet—
now we talk and talk

"Come home"
we cry to his soul—
lightning on the mountain

ON THE OLD BATTLEFIELD

Burning incense
in the treads of the tank
that crushed our lines

To the old marines
1,000 *dong* lunch money and a salute
from schoolboys

Beneath the mountain of battle
here on the flooded plain
only the sun burning

Marine Corps birthday:
"From the Halls of Montezuma…"
glowing incense – birthday candles

"Suck it up, Marine!"
gurgling from the *Behnar* * jug
sweet rice wine

Behnar is one of the 54 indigenous mountain tribes of Viet Nam

NIGHT STORM
Dong Ha

Wind rattling through the palm fronds,
raindrops exploding against my window,
chickens squawking as they scurry for shelter,
water buffalo huddling in a living fist,
sand grains sweeping across the naked highway,
the last empty bar locking its doors,
our manager turning out the hotel lights,
bellboys huddling over poker in the dark lounge,
my curtain floating on the breeze
leaking through my locked window —
these dwell among the ten thousand ways.
The earth quakes at the coming of the dragon.

THE OLD DMZ -
THE DEMILITARIZED ZONE

The 17th parallel and the Ben Ha River
once separated Viet Nam into North and South
and was a place of extreme violence during
both the French and American Wars

DMZ

The open belly
of the rusting fire dragon
sprouting pink blossoms

Rubble of a school —
gray-haired classmates toast and vow
"friendship forever"

Tall guard towers
staring across the river
manned by spiders

Begging forgiveness
as his feet first touch the North
his tears water earth

Our bombs stole his ears —
speaking what he cannot hear
his hands beat like wings

The bunker's sandbags
where her father ducked mortars
muffles her sobs

Rusting plane wreckage –
standing sentinel
two dark mountain children

Smiling black eyes
dawning above his gift
a purple balloon

By falling waters
a single lotus flower
a hand in prayer

THE KITE
Nan, on the border

Monsoons of burning metal
scalded our next harvest.
We could not eat ash.
I saw my family across the river.
Their rice was ashen too.
We could not meet, could not help each other,
could not even send a message
through the blazing muzzles lining both banks.
A postcard took a year and traveled
through a half dozen countries just to say,
"I am alive. I miss you. Please be well."
Finally I made a rice paper dragon,
tied it to a long string, hung a note from its talons.
Dragon floated on currents above the brown waters.
Dragon dodged and ducked burning missiles.
Dragon floated above my parents' hut.
Then I cut the string. Dragon tumbled home.
In this way, though the Powers denied us,
Dragon, wind, and I wished my weary aging parents,
Chuc muon nam moui. Happy New Year.

IN QUANG TRI PROVINCE

At the temple gate
empty stomach, bare gray head,
cone hat begging bowl

The grizzled old man
stooping in his cone hat shade
counting mini-vans

Yoga in the street –
she stretches, breathes deeply,
struggles not to cough

Mickey Mouse and Donald masks –
a gaggle of laughing children
dancing in traffic

Sipping jasmine tea –
last year's family coffee shop –
this year's hotel lounge

"What do you study?"
a chorus of bright-eyed youth
chant "tourism!"

Old green rivers and red hearts
stained with sorrow
and calm acceptance

Blossoming lotus
unseen in the hotel pond
announcing Buddha

MY VIETNAMESE DAUGHTER

FOR NGUYEN THI NGOC

7

THE RED BICYCLE

First meeting in Ha Noi, 2005

On this red bicycle—
wobbly wheels, broken spokes, rusted frame—
loaded with heavy sacks of rice and bullets
months to peddle south then back
my aunt struggled down muddy trails.

On this red bicycle
my thin legs and small hands steer and strain for hours
under my load of schoolbooks, questions, hope,
down strange streets, between cyclos, motorbikes, fumes
to be sure I do not miss you.

HUNG YEN

Ngoc's Que Huong* about 60 km southeast of Ha Noi

Midnight

In this crumbling stone hotel
we are tonight's only guests.
Through its tall archway
outside our shuttered windows
fog and cricket song.

In the Dark

The only moon this black and heavy night
is a distant farmer's bobbing lantern
as he picks his way through mud and dung

Dawn

Sky, mist, rice paddies
a single sheet of dull gray
wrinkled by white ducks

**Que Huong is the ancestral village where ancestors and roots can
go back thousands of years*

Fishing
10-year-old Hao

My friends study in school
while I trudge home from the village pond
with my empty pail

Landscape

Gray clouds, gray buildings
horizon to horizon
black eyes, sunlight smiles

HIGH AND DRY
Hoi An

The Dragon's mouth spurts, drawing
a soaked gauze curtain between us
and the teeming world beyond.
The Thu Bon River overflows its banks.
Sampans and tour boats float above the street.
The waters climb the stairs below
while hosts and helpers mop and bail.
My daughter and I sit on a terrace,
sipping mango, sharing rice and soup,
a simple meal on simple wooden planks.
We are dry behind the gauze and under a roof
with leaks that drip and plop beside us.
We are high for this single hour above these waters
that bring endless toil to the human flood
and tears from its endless surge.

LANGUAGE LESSONS
Hue

The broad sky and wide river
fade into a single blanket of darkness.
The steaming air cools.
Outside our window the neon lights and blaring music
of a reborn town awaken.
We pull the blanket over our toes
and snuggle into the deepening dark.

We open our volume of prison poetry
written by Bac Ho * while encased in hunger and gloom.
We read of toil and no water, lost teeth and friends,
but laugh as she cannot pronounce "z"
and I choke on "ng."

Together in the small quiet room
our prison bars are thrown open. Dawn bursts.
We share a family blanket that is all we need
to chase the shadows of history from our hearts.

*Bac means Uncle. Ho Chi Minh is affectionately called Bac Ho
by the entire country.

LETTER TO MY DAUGHTER
AFTER VISITING MY LAI

Yesterday we walked side-by-side
and hand-in-hand through the petrified prints
of the bare feet of fleeing mothers and children
and the stomping combat boots of marauding GIs.
We stood in the kitchen of ghosts.
We hugged before the hats, shirts, canes
of those who no longer use them.
I felt such shame. I could no longer feel
worthy to be your father. But all you did
was wipe my tears and call me *Bo*. *

That cane, that hat, were worn by an old man
who walked into your sleep last night.
Terror in his eyes, last prayer on his lips,
he came with the one who married him forever—
the GI you saw beating, beating, beating
his head, his face, his arms, his body.
This morning your own head screams with his pain.
His eyes are behind your eyes.
This morning as my fingers try to squeeze your ache away
I see his wounds, his blood,
breaking through your gentle almond face.

You cannot stand the pain of your grandfather
or the long suffering of your country.
I cannot stand the pain of my daughter
or the endless shame of my nation.
Side-by-side, hand-in-hand,
we carry this pain together.
Side-by-side, incense between our palms,
we bow as one before the altar of the dead.

*Bo is father in Vietnamese

146

Tears

My almond-eyed daughter
wipes the tears
of the sleep-sour veteran
then wrings her handkerchief
into the reservoir
in the heart of the world.

On Lang Co Beach

My large white bony fingers
knit with your small soft yellow ones.
We twine a multicolored knot
as we walk through scalding sands
toward the ocean's foam.
A butterfly leads the way.

HA NOI

THE NORTH

8

HA NOI

HA NOI DAWN

The golden crow spreads its wings
to rise between the tall gray buildings
throwing their long shadows across Truc Bach Lake.
Two small fishing boats with barely enough room
for their squatting elders
float between green hyacinth clumps.
A craggy boulder breaks and ripples the waters
like the back of a giant tortoise.
Bubbles percolate and pop on the surface
of the dark mirror like the breath
of that tortoise who is guardian of this city.
Elders stretch, dance, play badminton without nets.
Vendors spread their old clothes, dozen watches, pirated CDs,
snails and crabs and squirming fish.

I cross the trafficked street to stand in the grass of
    West Lake's bank.
I arrive as the sun's rays fall on the statue
marking the old pilot's descent and capture. *
A teen parks his moped at the stone man's feet.
No one notices him or me.

*Site of John McCain's crash landing over Ha Noi during his
23rd bombing raid in October 1967. He was wounded and saved
from drowning when a Vietnamese peasant dove into the lake
to rescue him.

That day and this are just two
of three hundred thousand Ha Noi dawns.
The golden crow will rise again
tomorrow and tomorrow and tomorrow,
but I must turn to face the sun
and walk another road that points in only one direction.
The high crow burns and laughs
as I leave the still waters behind
and plunge into the human tide.

TRAFFIC

Sun cracks the gray haze
on this ocean of mopeds
in fish-school thickness

The flower market—
rainbow shapes and colors
on her rusty bike

Chickens graze and peck
in their twisted wire cages
between crowded lanes

Smiling at Tai Chi
on the small cement island
in this traffic smog

Her fan-shaped black hair
waving like dark rice grasses
from her swift moped

SONG OF A GRIEVING MOTHER

Ngan, mid-70s rural northern woman

I love our water buffalo as much as our hut
and our vegetable patch as much as your school.
I love our rice paddy as much as my husband
and my father's tomb as much as my sleeping mat.
I love your father as much as our son.
I love our pig though we must eat him.
I love our star fruit, jackfruit, and mangoes.
I love rice, whether grass, seed, or grain.
I love you, my daughter, as my mother loved me.
No difference between these; this is *que huong.*
And so, my daughter, you and our country
are one and the same, no life without each.
And that is why, with a love more than love,
I dress you in bombs and kiss you as you leave.

SUMMER WINDS

After a painting by Pham Hau, 1940, in the Fine Arts Museum

I am a red dragonfly
clinging to the swaying stem
of a blossoming lotus

I am a speckled frog
content beneath lotus leaves
bending and dripping with rain

I am a broad green leaf
bowing my wide lobes
to ripple and kiss the pond

One white petal is torn off by the wind
I am that petal
flying away

Ha Noi Haiku and Tanka

Pottery

These million shards
scattered in the mud and dust
slice open my heart.
Thick incense fumes form clouds.
My prayers both bleed and rise.

The Flutist

Empty eye sockets—
his fingers see the air holes
on his bamboo flute

Dusk

Through the speckled mist
in the shadowed pagoda
in soft candlelight
smiling saffron-robed monks
chant our aching hearts home.

Flower Vendor
Co-written with Tran Dinh Song and Kate Dahlstedt

Midnight is my dawn
Flower markets never sleep
I doze at sunrise

TURTLE
Ngoc Son Pagoda*

If you see a turtle in the lake—blessed.
If you see a turtle in your dreams—thrice blessed.
If you see this turtle in his glass tomb
where he rests preserved in stillness
like the bearded uncle across the city
you are what you are and what you bring.

The old ones pray. The young take photos.
The foreigners point and gab.
I sit. I stare. I open the door in my chest
rusted shut by the old pains of this place
and by the eternal pain we all carry.
I bring it all to Turtle.

On a distant mountain, in my dreams,
crawling across the stone of this pagoda floor
I have seen turtle. In the temple on his stele
I kowtow, rub his marble head, lean forehead to forehead.
In this lake of thick green waters
I watch and watch the ripples and bubbles.

Gray dawn, early and quiet. The ant swarms are at rest.
Six grandmothers chant. Distant gongs sound.
This dawn the chorus of chirping sparrows
out-sings the din of motorbikes and taxis.

**The Jade Mountain Pagoda on the Lake of the Sword Restoration
where the body of a giant turtle rests. See Kim Quy for the full story.*

I hear myself breathing. I feel turtle's lungs
contract and expand, close and open, blossom.

As I bid farewell to this holy place
my limbs grow flippers and claws.
My nose becomes a snout. My mouth waters
with the taste of fish. Ripples. Ripples.
Now I must swim around the world.
Alone I am never alone.

THE NORTHERN COUNTRYSIDE AND COAST

FIRST MEETING

Nguyen, in the northern countryside

I saw the steel bird fall from the sky,
wings on fire, a phoenix dying.
Beneath a silken cloud and spider strands
only a boy floated to earth.
Through the smoke of our burning grasses
I looked into his rolling eyes,
bloodied face, trembling hands.
He too had a mother in grief.
I laid down my scythe. I fed him some rice.
I washed and wrapped his torn skin
then sent him in an ox cart to Ha Noi.

CHILDHOOD IN THE NORTH

Anh, son of an NVA soldier from the northern countryside

Soon after I learned my first words—
"mother," "father," "when," and "where"—
I strung them together like colored ribbons
making the tail of a fluttering kite.

"Where is my father?" I asked.
"He is a soldier," she said.
"When, Mother, will he come home?"
"Go out with the other children," she said,
"And watch for a man with a backpack
dusty and tired from his long walk home."

We played beneath the old banyan tree
where all the roads I knew joined as one.
I hid from my friends, scratched faces in the dirt,
waddled with ducks and looked down lanes.

Finally one day beneath a burning sun
the man with the backpack came.
I ran to him, grabbed his leg, held tight.
"Where is your home?" his gentle voice asked.
He was gone so long he must have forgotten.

We hobbled together, me with a father,
he like a man with a wooden leg.
He pried and pleaded but I would not let go.
Mother had to peel me off
like the skin of an unripe fruit.

I watched his backpack bouncing
as he disappeared down the long road.
Mother cried and begged forgiveness.
She said she had teased me, said she had lied,
said she was sorry, many had died.
It was then that I learned and have never forgotten
the pain with no answer in the little word "why?"

LEARNING THE LANGUAGE

My water buffalo
understands when I command
right, left, stop, or go.
You work hard to learn our tongue.
You are as fluent as my cow

RECONCILIATION

"As life flows on and on..."—Hat, disabled NVA Veteran

Toss a grenade
into my fishpond –
harvest the dead

My village
the fishpond
for your bombers

My friends,
family, children –
burnt rice

Our river
our survivors
their monsoon of tears

The white-haired white man
tears dripping
in our village mud

Love
dead
here

FUNERAL
Thiep, Hung Yen

"Here," he said to the Unfriendly Ones,
"I toss you white and purple petals.
I toss you sweets and paper money.
I gift you goods and goodies of this world
to carpet this road to our cemetery.
I implore you to let us pass
so that my mother's soul does not run off
stolen, seduced, or kidnapped by you.
Let her arrive with her body and with us
so that we may with incense and song
lay her in her final bed of earth."

Bamboo Speaks

From under the green waters
of our tiny family pond,
from between the whiskered catfish
and beneath the golden ducks,
I watch the moon cycle thirteen times
from full to empty to full again.
In this still place I grow hard and strong.
Soon I will emerge.
My family will eat with my chopsticks.
Our daughter will play me as her flute
and awaken the soul of our rice.

HA LONG REVERY*

The prow of my boat drifts east, drifts west,
crossing the face of the ragged mountain
whose countless crags sprout greenery
like the pores of a wizened elder's chin.
Above the jagged peaks – rising, falling, rising –
variegated gray and blue clouds float west, float east,
moving as slowly and steadily against my prow
as prow against mountain. Beneath these heavens,
thick green waters, impenetrable to sight,
wiggle and gurgle and glisten.
I am alone on deck between shifting plates
of water, earth, and sky. I seem to stand
on the only still place in the eternal grinding
of wind and current and time.
It is the grand illusion.
I pass. Sea, mountains, sky remain.
Yet for this moment I rejoice
to cling to the anchor in the center of all
that does not shift or drift or decay.

*Ha Long Bay, a world heritage site on the coast east of Ha Noi near
Hai Phong.

LULLABY

Because you are far away, my son,
and I am an old woman alone,
I listen in my quiet hours
to raindrops flicking lotus petals.
In this way, though you are gone, the patter
of your tiny feet fills my empty home.

ANGUISH AND ANSWER

Anguish

I writhe like a worm
crushed under ten thousand heels
while your flower sings.

Buddha's answer

Can you hear the song
of the upright lotus
soothing broken hearts?

You must die and die
ten thousand times and more
for your ears to open.

How else dissolve
the glue that fastens you
to this false world?

My blessing for you
is to know this, and to slay you
until you learn to laugh.

THE MEETING

A dragon rises from the Eastern Lake.
An eagle rises from the Western Mountain.
A common ocean laps their shores
and they soar in the same sky.

When east meets west
and west meets east
which way is west
and where is the east?

KIM QUY:

THE GOLDEN TORTOISE

THE TALE OF KING LE LOI

9

INTRODUCTION

MYTHS AND LEGENDS simultaneously record history, reveal psychology, preserve and promote culture, and illuminate and guide a people's spirit and soul. When we grasp myth, we discover what is universal, find ourselves in it, and truly become friends, as what was foreign becomes another home.

King Le Loi was one of the great figures of Vietnamese history and legend. His tale has remarkable similarities to heroic tales and foundational myths from all over the world. In the English-speaking world, it has special similarities to the stories of both King Arthur and George Washington. Like Arthur's it is complete with a magical sword akin to Excalibur and a golden tortoise akin to the Lady of the Lake. Like both Arthur's and Washington's, it is a story of a man of the land whose destiny was difficult and unknown, who led a tortured but heroic rebellion for freedom, became the freed people's ruler, and united fractionalized regions into one country and vision. All these legends transmit the themes of divine guidance and purpose, eternal friendship, personal and national identities defamed, discovered, and restored, and the struggle to build a legitimate, independent, and just country during both war and peace.

The culture hero's daunting and harmonizing adventure is the essence of the epic form, and it is universal. Herein Le Loi tells his Vietnamese tale in English language epic verse. His efforts help reconcile and unite what history and politics sundered.

Notes accompany the poem to guide readers in understanding Vietnamese myths, history, and customs that are detailed in the poem and in comparing this myth with others of similar theme and content. Some details vary in different versions of Le Loi's myth. Such variations always occur in myths derived from the oral tradition. I first heard many parts of this tale verbally retold by friends, guides, teachers, and acquaintances in various regions of Viet Nam. All versions are true to the integrity and coherence of the story and its cumulative vision and message. We are all invited to give our swords to the Golden Tortoise and build peace, reconciliation, and friendship between our nations and all peoples.

KIM QUY: THE GOLDEN TORTOISE
The tale of King Le Loi

1

I lived in a hut near the turbulent sea.
Daily as I fished, the dragon's tail whipped foam in my face.
Nightly as I tossed, the dragon's breath rustled my
thatched roof.
It seemed to be restless. It seemed to be calling.
It seemed to be crying. It had not given birth
to one hundred children, nor spoken to kings,
so that we would carry the names of slaves.[1]
I thought I could hear this but I was afraid.
I was just a poor fisherman. What could I do? [2]

Not now but more years than the scales on a dragon—
not now but more years than we tend our ancestors—
that long the invaders had eaten our rice,
stolen our children, forced us to use their words
and their alphabet, called our home Pacified,
a slave name with no honor.[3] In mountains and villages
my brothers rebelled, sharpened bamboo,
chipped stones, shaped bows. In small bands and large
they bid farewell to their wives and children
and charged and fought or dodged and hid.[4]

But I seemed made of bones, my wife and children
all bones. It was all I could do, year upon year,
to haul my sampan to the sea, to row
against tides, to drag my nets through surf
and dump their load on the deck of my boat.

I looked with longing at my rebel brothers.
My heart shed tears for their vacant huts.
My blood boiled oil when the invaders
torched a neighbor's home or snatched my catch
to feed their hoards that chained our land.

When the Emperor cries out, we must not refuse.
My heart beat like grandfather's bronze drum
when he called the dragon to bring the rains.[5]
I tossed in the nights. I towed through the tides.
I hauled my nets though shivering from toil.
One night the dragon's roar boiled the moon.
I did not sleep, yet weary I rowed,
weary I tossed, weary I hauled the net
that seemed to grow heavier, as if the sea
would drag me in and make me its food.

So be it, I thought. Let the dragon eat me.
Free me from slavery. Make me your egg.
So be it! My heart gave up. One final yank
would swallow me. I pulled my last pull
against tide and foam, glad to drown quickly
and not be a slave. But instead of swallowing
the dragon spit. Like a flying moon,
my tangled net leapt from the sea.
I kowtowed as it clanged on the deck.
This is how gods speak. Then who am I?

2[6]

I untangled the strange iron blade from my net.
For weeks I stared as it lay on my altar

where I had placed it before my father,
grandfather, and his father too.[7]
I lit extra incense, the odd number three
that we give to the spirits when all is in question.[8]
I asked them to speak and answer the riddle—
tell me the meaning of this blade from the sea.
The dragon continued to roar day and night,
crying its pain. But it did not answer.

Far worse than not knowing what to do
is not doing what one knows one must.
Far worse than not knowing who one is
is feeling a destiny that will not unfold.
Our sea is our dragon, our ancestor, our sperm.
Our sea calm and stormy is worshipped forever
as father of our people. The sea had spit forth
a tool not of my trade by a warrior's.
If Father could only rage against slavery
then Mother, dear Mother, might guide her lost son.

I turned to the mountains where the fairy lives.
I turned to the mountains whose clouds are their crowns,
whose gray mist is breath, whose jungles are cloaks
of green swathing for our fairy mother's arms.
She too had been silent, breathing in pain.
Her tea plants were broken, their leaves unreadable.
Into her jungle of thick hanging vines,
of mud paths and swamps, of snakes and bats,
I plunged, I pushed, I plodded without rice.
Answer me, Mother! Who is your son?

In deep jungle darkness where I breathed green air,
where steep slopes are made of slick green rocks,

where before me only fairies dare tread,
there in the green air where Earth breathed her sorrow,
no food in my belly, no hope in my chest,
in the midst of a grove of emerald-leafed bamboo,
poles longer, more sections, than bamboo can grow,
a light, a golden light not of this world
shone like the sun buried in earth,
shone like the breath of the Mother herself.[9]

Again I bowed deeply, this time to Mother.
The light seemed to shine through my palms and it
burned.
I clutched. I coiled. I became like the snake
churning through soil to escape from all threat.
Loam flew from my fingers, and grubs and roots,
until deep in Earth's body my fingers hit metal,
firm and cool, long and true, shaped to a purpose.
Mother threw me the sheath of a warrior
inscribed with two names, my best friend's and mine,
followed by titles I dared not utter.[10]

3

Home again. Home again. Legs flying home.
Down rock slopes. Through mangroves. Past woodcutters'
huts.
I clutched the dank bundle, my gift from the earth.
I did not know or guess the Emperor's purpose
but as I ran and stumbled and ran once more
I saw in clear light that the Land and the Water—
the name of our country, elements of our parents—
cried as they rattled the chains of our slavery.[11]

At home without food, without thought, without fear
I fell before the altar of all we hold dear.

Incense wafting, ancestors fed, wife worried for my life
reassured and asleep, I took out the casing
from beneath my rags. I stroked it and hugged it
and read it once more. My name and my friend's
in letters of gold—like the light, like the breath,
like the heart of the dragon. My fingers
trembled as I lifted it high. My heart
halted between past and future, despair and elation,
enslavement and action. One final prayer
and I lifted the sword. Of its own it leapt home.

A sword in its scabbard is a heart in its home,
a people on their land, a dream in its act.
Still I dared not speak. For days my family
had had no fish, for weeks I had seemed strange.
Now I began to believe the impossible
and went in search of the friend of my youth.[12]
Far wiser than I, with eyes made of onyx,
a mind like a mountain river in spring,
he listened in silence, he nodded, he prayed.
When the Emperor speaks, we dare not refuse.

My friend said to wait and sent me home.
He told me to fish in the sea and the river.
He told me to watch – when dragon was ready
we should be ready. Until then the sword
must hide its prediction in a poor man's rags.
He went to the mountains with buckets of honey
and the tiny brushes made for a scholar.
While I fished, while I watched, while dragon still
screamed,

he lettered the sweet words found on the scabbard
in dripping bee's gold on hundreds of leaves.

Ants are the soldiers and workers who teach
how to build villages and cities as one.
Ants found the honey. Ants ate the letters.
Ants who build cities now wrote the words
announced by the mountain, spoken by sea,
into the leaves of the forest in fall.
Wise friend! Winds blew. Cold climbed the hills.
Leaves fell, floated, tumbled, shod the feet
of our people. Now everyone knew. Miracle
of shrewdness, his first public deed.

4

The people rose up, chains of fear snapped,
and marched to my village an army of ants.
They cried my name, insisted I lead.
Only then did I take the sword from my rags,
only then strap it on, only then tell the tale.
The dragon will lead us, the mountain give strength,
the sword of the two made one by their children.
Freedom was born then, long before battle.
Freedom was born in the dream of a people
chained too long by kings with no love.

Battle is horror. I never will praise it.
I always felt pity for each fish I took.
Invaders were many with their wagons and swords.
We remembered their cruelty of twelve hundred years.
The sword led the way with its power and its light.

180

It was not I and I never will claim it.
The words of the mountain, the blade of the sea,
the dream of a people, the faith of a friend,
these became one as one became dragon
and carved through all trouble. Our enemies fled.

I established my kingdom, friend by my side,
like a smashed porcelain teapot with love restored,
all people welcome from city and shore,
all dragon's children from the same bag.
We sowed and we built, we sang and made laws.
I stayed near the sea to remember the tides.
I traveled to mountains, jungles, and plains,
villages, hamlets, collecting all strays,
making us one as ants are one colony,
all dragon's children from the same bag.[13]

I ever loved fishing. I always loved fish.
I studied the currents and tested the waters.
Wearing the sword of the Emperor of Water
I never forgot who I was by myself.
One night on a boat above the Red River,
stars blazing like scales on a great dragon's flanks,
my friend beside me, my guards all around,
I lowered my king's body to the hard wooden planks.
As close as I could stoop to my origins
I kowtowed forehead to deck to give thanks.

My people say that when we see a dragon
in dreamtime it means the Emperor gives nod.
Some call it a dream, for others no name
but a vision of something more real than life.
Bowed to the ground of the lake in my boat

I saw what our King saw rise from the deep.
Scales of gold, wings of flame, eyes of sparkling jade,
the dragon leapt from water to sky.
His tail and his wake wrote across heaven
that our people and freedom would never die.

5

Here, said my friend, I must build my center.
So there I planted temples, schools, and laws
till they grew and they glowed like new young rice.
When invaders stampede on our rice and our dreams
future rulers will wield the soul of my sword.
The dragon will guide them forever to rise.
Rising Dragon showed it. Our king named it for him.
The rice was now ours. Our home was now free.
Contented, I boarded my old wooden boat.
Contented, I floated beneath a full moon.

The lake was a looking glass kissed by a goddess.
The sky showed the sparkle of the great dragon's teeth.
My friend by my side, our rowers all nodding,
I thought all was done, I thought rest was mine.
But I have learned this from the hardships of fishing,
of war, and of ruling—never think yourself done.
Relax in a calm sea—a storm will soon follow.
Think yourself safe and your throne may be lost.
Beneath the calm surface that mirrored my kingship
of old I heard the dragon roil and cry.

A great pointed head broke the lake's surface.
Like the scales of a dragon, a huge shell appeared.

Did I sin? Lose faith? I thought it a monster
and grabbed the strong hilt of my sword from the sea.
I raised it high as I had against Ming.
It flashed in the moon and my name flashed with light.
I was ready to strike to protect the dragon
so long forced to wear the chains of a slave.
Pointing to the sky, I gathered my power
of casting and seeking, of striking and building.

"Oh King," cried a voice of thunder and jasmine.
"Great Emperor," cried my heart in terror and awe.
"Do not strike," said the sky through the mouth of the
turtle.
The tortoise stared into me with eyes like the sword—
piercing, invincible, cutting to bone.
I remembered the sea that first threw the blade.
I remembered the mountain that first cried my name.
Sea dragon our father, mountain fairy our mother—
tortoise is created of mountain and sea.

I watched turtle's green shell become golden,
golden his beak, claws, tail, and sharp eyes.
Under the moon all my city was pale
while tortoise radiated the ancient gold light.
I saw at once that all that we are
are pale shadows of truth, shades of a will
that runs through all time and composes all tales
that we must enact to assist the one king.
In turtle's mouth I placed my great sword.
More than God gives us, we must return.

NOTES TO *KIM QUY*

The tale of King Le Loi

1   The dragon is the ruling spirit and ancestral father of the Viet people. He is Long Quan, Dragon King, Emperor of the Waters, whose realm is the sea. The myth of the origins of the Vietnamese people is that Long Quan married Au Co, the mountain fairy, who gave birth to 100 eggs in one sack. These hatched into their children. 50 children returned to the mountains with Au Co, becoming the indigenous mountain tribes of Viet Nam. 50 returned to the sea with Long Quan, becoming the Viet people. Viet Nam literally means Country of the Southern Viets.

2   Some versions of the myth say that Le Loi was originally a poor fisherman. Historically, it is believed that he was a landowner from Thanh Hoa province south of Ha Noi. The fisherman is also said to have been *Le Than*, who later gave Le Loi the sword blade as leader of the rebellion.

3   The Chinese name for Viet Nam was Annam, which means The Pacified South. The Chinese occupied Viet Nam for almost 1,200 years, from 179 BCE to 938 CE. For centuries following the initial liberation, the Chinese invaded again and again, sometimes occupying parts of Viet Nam for periods of time and over centuries absorbing the northern Viet people.

Historically, Le Loi's rebellion was against an especially cruel 20-year occupation by the Ming Dynasty, 1407-1427. Le Loi claimed kingship in 1418 and led a rebellion that lasted 10 years, ending with a major victory over the Chinese in 1428. This initiated the Le Dynasty, Viet Nam's longest and most stable ruling dynasty, which retained power until 1788.

4   In Viet Nam neighboring villagers are addressed as older or younger brothers or sisters. Every man who rebelled was engaging his entire family. Vietnamese people do not think of themselves as autonomous units; they do not act for themselves but for their community, nation, and ancestors.

5   Bronze drums have been found in Vietnamese archeological digs dating back to the Bronze Age before 1,000 BCE. During droughts farmers

would beat their drums to notify the beneficent dragon spirit of their need for rain.

6 In some versions the Golden Tortoise appears early to give Le Loi the sword as well as later to retrieve it.

7 Vietnamese have practiced ancestor veneration since archaic times. Every household has an altar to the ancestors where family members light incense, pray, leave food offerings, and council with the spirits of their departed. Families venerate their ancestors going back four generations, a full century, and live with the confidence that they will be honored the same way in the future – "Our children are our social security."

8 Folk tradition holds that incense sticks are lit in odd numbers, and three are lit when we have a particular question to put before the spirits.

9 Some versions say that rather than digging, Le Loi saw the light in a banyan tree, climbed it, and found the sword's missing piece.

10 Some say it was the hilt rather than the scabbard. And versions differ as to the exact wording on the sword. Some say it read, "By the Will of Heaven." In all versions the message is similar to the Arthurian prediction of "the Once and Future King."

11 Vietnamese refer to their country as *dat nuoc*, The Land and the Water, demonstrating the essential unity of elements necessary to sustain an agricultural people.

12 Le Loi's "wise friend" was poet, Confucian, and counselor Nguyen Trai, respected as Viet Nam's greatest mandarin. He advised Le Loi, "It is better to conquer hearts than citadels." Their early friendship is poetic invention.

13 Vietnamese refer to all their people, Viet and indigenous, as *dong bao,* "children from the same bag." This refers to their common origins as the 100 eggs born in the sack of the dragon and the fairy. To great acclaim, Ho Chi Minh used the phrase in his 1945 address to the Vietnamese people declaring independence.

14 The original name of Ha Noi is Thang Long, which means Rising or Ascending Dragon. In 1010 King Ly Thai Tho had the vision of a golden

dragon rising from a lake, moved his capital to the site, and named it Thang Long. Le Loi's capital was also at Thang Long, but he called it Dong Kinh, Royal Capital of the East. It was renamed Ha Noi, meaning City in the River Bend, City in the Middle of the Waters, or City Amidst the Waters, by Emperor Ming Mang when he moved the capital back from Hue in the nineteenth century. Le Loi re-experiencing the vision of the ascending dragon is poetic invention.

In honor of Le Loi's meeting with the golden tortoise, the lake in the center of Ha Noi is named Ho Hoan Kiem, Lake of the Sword Restoration. Giant turtles have still lived in it until recent times, occasionally being seen and bringing good omens.

In 1963 the dead body of a giant turtle was recovered from the lake. It was over 6 feet long and 3 feet wide and weighed about 500 pounds. Its age was estimated to be 500 years, dating back to the era of the historical Le Loi and his successful decade-long rebellion against the Ming occupation. 1963 was a time of American escalation of the war in Viet Nam, which would last another decade. The discovery of this turtle and its connection to the legend of Le Loi was received as spiritual encouragement to resist the contemporary invaders. The skeleton on the turtle can be viewed at the Ngoc Son Temple of the lake today. This Jade Mountain Temple rises out of the Sword Restoration Lake and is accessible by an arching red wooden foot bridge. At its base stands an altar to the God of Literature, honoring the power of poetry and writing to defend, preserve, and heal. There the tortoise rests.